Grand Rapids Then and Now

by
James VanVulpen
Contemporary Photographs by Rex Larsen

Published by
The Grand Rapids Historical Commission

Printed by
West Michigan Printing, Inc.
840 Ottawa NW
Grand Rapids, Michigan 49503

Edited and designed by
Editorial Consultants
2215 Oak Industrial Drive NE
Grand Rapids, Michigan 49505

Table of Contents

Acknowledgments. iv

Foreword v

Prologue: "A Window Through Time". . . . 1

Grand Rapids City Boundaries, Then
and Now 13

Tour Map and Guide to Photographs . . 14-15

Grand Rapids Then and Now, A Statistical
Comparison. 16

The Photographs: Grand Rapids
Then and Now. 17

Acknowledgments

Production of a book involves many people. The author wishes particularly to thank the members of the Grand Rapids Historical Commission: John Logie, president; Micki Benz, Harold Dekker, Mary Edmond, Leo W. Graff, Jr., June Horowitz, Margaret Snow, Albert Steil, Anthony Travis, Francisco Vega, Mary Alice Williams, and Ronald Yob. The Historical Commission funded publication of this volume with a loan from the Grand Rapids Foundation.

City Historian Gordon Olson, who had charge of the book's publication, has been patient and resourceful beyond the call of duty during the long period of preparation. Ellen Arlinsky, editor, and Marg Ed Kwapil, designer, of Editorial Consultants, have done their usual fine job. Credit must also be given to Celene Idema for her neat preparation of the 1876 map, and to Chris Gray for the numbered guide map.

Finally, special thanks are due to the Rev. Dennis Morrow, without whose unfailing interest and encouragement the idea for *Grand Rapids Then and Now* might never have become a reality.

J. V.

Foreword

The pages of this book provide a kind of "window" through time. Through it, with the help of a little imagination, your eyes can gaze backward exactly one hundred years upon a fragment of vanished America, reflected in the streets of one Midwestern city.

The photographic views on the left-hand pages beginning on page 18 were all taken in the spring of 1888 at various locations around Grand Rapids. Those on the facing pages were shot from exactly the same spots (or as nearly as possible, in some instances) in the spring of 1988. The result is a fascinating juxtaposition — two slices of "time present" upon identical frames of space, at a one-hundred-year interval.

The contemporary photographs were taken by the award-winning *Grand Rapids Press* photographer Rex Larsen. Long hours of research, however, have failed to turn up the name of the nineteenth-century photographer or photographers who hauled cumbersome apparatus around the city to produce the original pictures. First collected by the International Publishing Company and printed in a book entitled *Grand Rapids Illustrated,* the 1888 photographs were accompanied by a brief written sketch of the city, a "puff" piece, which we have omitted here, written by local newspaperman Ernest B. Fisher. Several views from the 1888 book also had to be left out, either because they were redundant or because their location today is inaccessible — under an expressway, for instance.

The text accompanying this book has been researched among a variety of sources. Those most consulted include newspapers, memoirs, directories, published histories (notably Albert Baxter's *History of Grand Rapids, Michigan,* which was being written at the time the original photos were taken, and Z. Z. Lydens' 1966 volume, *The Story of Grand Rapids*), and a promotional booklet, *Grand Rapids As It Is,* printed in 1888 by the local Board of Trade and our source for two of the pictures shown in this book — the Harry Widdicomb house and the Phoenix furniture factory.

A lot of the remaining material comes from bits and pieces noted during years of looking up other things for other local history projects. Accuracy has been the constant goal, but if any errors of fact have slipped in, the author cheerfully takes responsibility.

Our photographs, originals on the left, contemporary on the right, are arranged in the order you might see them in the course of a full day of touring Grand Rapids. The originals were obviously taken over a period of weeks, as a look at the growth of tree leaves in various shots will show, but for the fun of it, we'll condense our imaginary visit into a single day. To guide us, on pages 14-15, is a numbered map of central Grand Rapids, indicating on present-day streets the locations shown in the pictures.

The commentary that accompanies the pictures conveys a sense of two simultaneous tours through the city, flashing back and forth between centuries. So let us step through our "window through time" and embark on a day's journey through two springtimes, just one hundred years apart.

Prologue

"A Window Through Time"

The Grand Rapids of 1988 is Michigan's second-largest city, three-time winner of the "All-America City" award. Covering an area of about forty-five square miles, the city of Grand Rapids along with its surrounding suburban communities of East Grand Rapids, Grandville, Kentwood, Walker, and Wyoming together add up to a population of close to 350,000.

Noted as the world's largest producer of office furniture, the city also boasts over a thousand other manufacturers turning out a widely diverse line of products. Gateway to West Michigan's popular tourist attractions, Grand Rapids still takes pride in being a city of homes and churches, a "good place to raise a family."

Small enough to be comfortable, large enough to be metropolitan, the city has produced nationally known authors, actors, artists, scientists, and statesmen — even a president of the United States. This is the city you'll see in our pictures on the right-hand pages.

Now, let's flash back just one hundred years.

Imagine that we're sitting in a railroad coach on the Grand Rapids and Indiana line, approaching the city from the south on a spring day in 1888, around the beginning of May. You are a first-time visitor, and I'm going to show you around. But first, I'd better tell you a little about this town and these times.

Grover Cleveland is president of the United States, and Queen Victoria still reigns over a British Empire preeminent in the world. There are only thirty-eight stars on the American flag. Hawaii is an independent kingdom, and Alaska is a territory. Nine other western territories in the "Lower Forty-eight" — Washington, Idaho, Montana, Wyoming, Dakota (still undivided into North and South), Utah, Arizona, New Mexico, and Indian Territory (later to be known as Oklahoma) — have yet to be admitted to the Union. Two-thirds of America's people live in rural areas, not cities.

Albert Einstein, Joseph Stalin, Franklin and Eleanor Roosevelt, and Harry Truman are small children in various places around the world. Adolf Hitler won't be born for another year, Dwight

Eisenhower for two, and Ronald Reagan for nearly a quarter-century.

In the words of a British novelist, "The past is a foreign country. They do things differently there." In Grand Rapids, as it would be in any other town, 1888 presents a strange appearance to the traveler from a hundred years in the future.

High button shoes and floor-length dresses with bustles are fashionable, and women wear their uncut hair piled high. Most men sport beards or mustaches, and their high hats, derbies, vests, suits, and frock coats look odd to us. Manners and written language, even speech, all seem stiffly formal.

Houses tend to be large and ornate, with towers, spires, and "gingerbread" decorating the residences of the more affluent. No movies, TV sets, VCRs, or stereos exist. "Talking machine" phonographs, with their hand cranks, scratchy cylinders, and horn-like acoustic speakers, provide the latest in home entertainment.

Horse-drawn carriages and wagons fill the streets. Bicycles have high front wheels and small rear ones. Locomotives have tall smokestacks and long, low boilers. Horses, steam engines, or human muscles power virtually every form of transportation.

The city limits of Grand Rapids, Michigan, in the County of Kent,

Wooden sprinkler carts helped keep the dust down on city streets.

extend just over nine square miles, and the population is around sixty thousand. Farms and woodlands occupy the land where one day incorporated suburbs will grow.

The town, only a generation removed from the frontier, is still a jumping-off place for the northern woods, with a lingering reputation as a rip-roaring lumberjack hangout. The quality of the home furniture produced here has just begun to be noted around the country in the past dozen years, but Grand Rapids has not yet been dubbed the "Furniture Capital of America." Still, one thing won't change substantially over the course of a century: As most 1880's residents will testify, Grand Rapids is a good place to raise a family.

We have on page 13 a map assembled from a set of maps published in 1876, showing the general layout of the city and its surroundings, extending from what eventually will be Knapp on the north, Alger on the south, Oakleigh on the west, and the Beltline on the east. All this land will be almost totally built over in a century.

The city line, running along Sweet (north), Eastern (east), Hall (south), and Garfield (west), remains in 1888 where it has been since 1861, and several working farms still lie within city limits. Most of the layout shown outside of town still holds true in 1888, but in the twelve years since the map was drawn, the built-up area has overflowed into platted developments. Many of the newest plats are on the southeast side of town, especially along Madison Avenue, which runs vertically up the map's center, and East Street (the future Eastern Avenue). The place that will soon become Madison Square, however, is still the Kent County Agricultural Fairgrounds — note its oval horse track on section six of Paris Township.

It's sometimes hard to tell the difference between country and town from the condition of the streets. The city contains 143 miles of them, with more than fifty-five miles being unimproved dirt roadways that are a dust hazard in dry weather and turn to quagmires when it rains. Another seventy-five miles' worth of streets are graveled, more than half with stone gutters added. Only about seven miles, primarily in the downtown area, are paved with wood — six-inch sections of cedar block, set on end and packed with sand. Cobblestone pavement totals perhaps a mile, mostly on steep hillsides. Asphalt paving won't begin here until 1890.

There is, by the way, no consistency in the designation of "Streets" and "Avenues." The Grand River is the demarcation line between east and west thoroughfares, but address numbers start wherever the street does, and one street's building numbers bear no relation to another's. Not until 1912 will a uniform numbering system be adopted and thoroughfares divided into north-south "Avenues" and east-west "Streets." Still, it's easier to find your way around in 1888 than it has been in previous years. City Marshal Charles S. Wilson and his crew of workmen have just finished putting up street signs, six hundred brass ones and six hundred made of wood, all around the city.

In addition to the railroad lines shown on the 1876 map, a new line, the Grand Rapids, Lansing and Detroit, incorporated in 1887, is under construction to the southeast and will open to traffic in July 1888. A broken line on the map indicates the right-of-way for this newest service into Grand Rapids, which will also have a spur going out to Reeds Lake. When completed, the Grand Rapids, Lansing and Detroit will make a total of ten rail routes serving the city from various directions. It will cut travel time to Detroit down to three hours and fifty minutes, the fastest rail time in the state. By July 1888, sixty-seven trains will pass through the city.

Railways are the lifeline connecting Grand Rapids to other cities. There aren't any highways worth the name, since state routes are little more than mere wagon roads, often poorly maintained. Reaching out into the countryside in various directions are eight privately owned gravel toll roads, which farmers prefer for hauling produce into the city to market. There are, incidentally, over five thousand farms in the county producing grains, fruits, livestock, and garden vegetables. With seven large steam- or water-powered mills producing hundreds of barrels of flour a day, the city has become an important milling center.

Though lumberjacks still walk the streets every spring after their annual log drives, numbers are down from a decade ago. Nearby timber has been almost exhausted. Facing the end of its lumbering era, the city has already begun developing a broad base of industry, dominated by furniture, which will shape its character well into the coming century. There are 382 factories by the latest count.

More local workers, by far, are employed in furniture manufacturing than in any other industry, but many individuals labor in other manufacturing lines. Ranked by number of workers, behind the sawmills and planing mills come makers of such wood-related products as carriages, wagons, barrels, tubs, pails, and carpet sweepers. Boiler and machine shops, railroad car shops, and tanneries each account for several hundred employees, and substantial numbers find work in brickyards, breweries, cigar companies, shoe factories, and plaster mills, according to a list from the Board of Trade.

To the twentieth-century visitor, the pace of life might seem idyllically slow next to our own, but the citizens of 1888 view themselves as bustling, progressive folk. The telephone is becoming less of a novelty than it was nine years ago, when the first Grand Rapids exchange opened. Now, in 1888, there are over a thousand telephones in the city; in less than a century there will be half a million.

Electric lights are also growing in popularity, although most homes

Workers at the Grand Rapids Refrigerator Company making cabinets for Leonard "Cleanable" refrigerators. By 1925 Grand Rapids Refrigerator was a national industry leader.

Harriet ("Aunt Hattie") Guild Burton.

are still lit by gaslight or oil lamps. The new City Hall has been built with both gas and electric fixtures, just to be fully up to date. Arc lights have been installed at many street corners since the local power company started the first hydroelectric plant in the nation, back in 1880.

Grand Rapids received its village charter from the state in April 1838 and is now celebrating its first half-century of municipal existence. In that time, a small frontier outpost has blossomed into a thriving city, whose sixty thousand citizens represent almost double the population of only a decade ago. And yet, many surrounding farms are still occupied by the settlers who originally cleared them from the wilderness. "Aunt Hattie" Burton, last survivor of Kent County's earliest family of Yankee settlers, is hale and hearty at age 75. Plenty of other old-timers are still around, and you can hear their firsthand accounts of pioneer days at the annual picnic held by the Old Residents' Association.

We can learn a lot about the Grand Rapids of 1888 by scanning its daily newspapers. A few years ago there were six; now there are four: the *Eagle,* the *Democrat,* the *Evening Leader,* and the *Telegram-Herald.* A dozen weekly journals also are published in Grand Rapids, some specializing in literature, science, politics, religion, trade, manufacturing, real estate and building, as well as general news. Four of these are printed in Dutch, two in German, and one in Swedish. But rather than explore them all, a glance through a few recent issues of one of the dailies should be enough to fill in some more details and give us a sense of local atmosphere.

Let's see. . . . Among the items in the "Brevities" column of last Sunday's — April 29th — *Eagle* is a note that Turkish and Russian baths are open at Monroe and Ionia streets. There's also happy news for lovers of street-corner music: "These warm and balmy days have started the band organ and the little German band." Another sure sign of spring is the announcement in the same column that open horse cars will be placed on the street railway lines "as soon as the new ones arrive, which will be in about two weeks." And here's something you don't see much of anymore, an item that harks back to the bountiful fishing of Indian days: "A sturgeon weighing one hundred and twelve pounds was caught in the Grand River yesterday and was on exhibition at 117 Monroe Street last night." Sturgeon will disappear from these parts in a few years.

One indication of a significant population trend in the city was also reported in the April 29th *Eagle*:

> When the Michigan Central train arrived in Grand Rapids yesterday afternoon, the population of the city was increased 150, for that was the number of Hollanders who were aboard two special cars. A baggage car full of bags, boxes, satchels and trunks soon covered the platform. The entire party was a happy lot; they ranged in age from the babe in arms to those who have seen 50 or 60 winters. The Union Depot for a while was fairly given up to them with no one to molest or make them afraid.

In fact, in 1888, almost a third of the city's population is foreign born. An overwhelming majority of the immigrants come from northern Europe — Irish, Germans, Scandinavians, Poles — with the Dutch leading them all. One need only note the existence of thirteen Reformed and Christian Reformed churches, in a city where most mainline denominations have no more than four or five, to see the thrust of the future.

An increasing number of Italians have settled on the south and southwest sides in recent years, and, to be honest, there have been instances of bigotry toward them. Other Mediterranean and eastern European natives are a tiny minority. Hardly any citizens of Oriental or Hispanic origin have yet come to live in this valley. Most of the Ottawa who lived here when the white men came were moved thirty years ago to reservations up north by terms of a treaty with the federal government. But the years will continue to bring many newcomers to the city, and racial and ethnic diversity will greatly enrich the Grand Rapids of 1988.

Black citizens have been in this area since early pioneer times, but fewer than a thousand live here in 1888. The great migration from the South will not begin until around World War II. Not for another eighty-five years will Grand Rapids have its first mayor of

Sturgeon like this 250-pounder were still occasionally taken from the Grand River in the 1880s and 1890s.

African descent, the Reverend Lyman Parks. However, a farmer out in Gaines Township, William J. Hardy, was chosen township supervisor back in 1872, the first black elected official in Michigan. One of Hardy's sons, Eugene, is a noted music teacher here in town and a popular orator at the annual Emancipation Day celebrations held by the black community.

Unfortunately, despite the successes of families like the Hardys, racism is a pervasive fact of life in the America of 1888, far worse than it will be in the late twentieth century. If we told Grand Rapids residents in 1888 that in exactly one hundred years, the Reverend Jesse Jackson would visit their city to seek votes in the Michigan presidential primary — and that he would win — they'd be astounded.

Back to the newspapers.... A front-page story in the *Eagle* of April 29 details the many improvements underway around the city. A large new livery stable is to be built at Wealthy and LaGrave. Several downtown buildings are being painted, and work has begun on some new business structures. The basement walls of the Fox brothers' new stone "castle" at Cherry Street and College Avenue are about finished. And "work is progressing quite rapidly on the Sherman Street sewer. This, when completed, will drain a large amount of property, and place in the market many choice residence lots."

There's no doubt that the building boom which has swept Grand Rapids during the 1880s isn't letting up. Construction of the Grand Rapids, Lansing and Detroit Railroad has spurred further expansion to the southeast. Oakdale Park (formerly the Calkins, Lonsbury, and Gould farms), situated on either side of East Street between Oak Hill Cemetery and the new tracks, is the latest suburb to spring up, and its growth seems phenomenal. According to the *Eagle,* the railroad has unloaded fifteen carloads of stone for new buildings there. Work is about to start on a factory near the tracks for the Michigan Fire Ladder and Truck Company, manufacturers of wooden ladders and fire wagons, and on a $4,000 depot near where the rails cross East Street.

Says the *Eagle*:

> Already there have been 1,000 shade trees set out at Oakdale Park, and the railroad company expects that the grounds surrounding the depot will be very handsome. An acre of land has been donated here by [developers] Weston & Meigs for park purposes. Building will commence in that vicinity in earnest in the morning, as several carloads of lumber are already on the ground.

Nearby, the article goes on, "Briggs & Stevens have lately platted forty acres of the Martin farm on East Street...making 220 lots. Among the names of the streets are Weston, Dickinson and Cleveland Avenues."

On the west side of town as well, according to an *Eagle* article two weeks ago,

> already the sounds of the hammer and saw are heard in all directions, and those who are up in figures estimate that there are now fifty new buildings going up, and they expect at least 500 more residences and blocks will be erected on that side before the season closes.

Hotels, stores, and factory additions are noted. "And now," the piece continues,

> another enterprise is to be added. The Grand Rapids School Furniture Company has under process of erection a commodious and substantial structure to be used as a manufacturing establishment. It is located on Broadway near Tenth Street and the walls are now completed as far as the second story.

In the next century, this seed will develop into the huge American Seating Company plant.

It seems obvious from all these news stories that Grand Rapids is a growing, prosperous town. However, it would be a mistake to conclude that this idyllic portrait is the whole picture. From a safe distance in the future, popular mythology will paint the nineteenth century in America as a "younger, more innocent time." In some senses, that may be true. Nineteenth-century citizens have not seen world wars, nuclear arms races, or the "sexual revolution." But human nature doesn't change very much in only a hundred years. Both its virtues and its vices may wear slightly different trappings, but close examination reveals that they remain remarkably constant over time.

Drug and alcohol abuse are common social problems in 1888, as they will be a century hence. An often-long list of drunks processed through Police Court is a regular feature in the daily newspapers. There are 115 licensed saloons within the city, plus numerous roadhouses outside city limits, especially around Reeds Lake, three miles east. An uncertain number of illegal liquor establishments are known to flourish as well. The human distress attributed to these places, legal and otherwise, provides ammunition for a growing segment of the public, which thinks that prohibition laws are the only answer.

Opium dens also operate in Grand Rapids. Cocaine is a common ingredient in over-the-counter patent medicines, and overdoses of morphine, which can be bought over the counter in any drugstore, are an everyday occurrence. Even absinthe, a potent liqueur flavored with wormwood, is available here; few people know it, but Lloyd Brezee, editor and proprietor of the *Herald,* is addicted to the drug, which will soon cost him control of his paper, and eventually his life.

A revealing comment on civic morality came a few months ago, when Police Superintendent Israel C. "Bub" Smith openly admitted that, in his opinion, brothels supervised by the police department are simply a "necessary evil."

> Where they have conformed to the rules and regulation of the department where they have not been molested. I consider that it is better to permit houses of prostitution to exist and run with open doors under police regulation than that the pure and chaste women of the city should be assaulted and insulted upon the streets, as I believe would be the case without these institutions.

The chief also admitted knowledge of several professional gambling dens operating in the city with little police interference.

These revelations have surfaced during the course of a hearing of charges by Smith against County Prosecuting Attorney Samuel D. Clay, alleging official misconduct. Clay's misfortunes have been providing the community with its juiciest local scandals of 1888. A successful lawyer, married to the first female doctor in Grand Rapids (Frances Rutherford, who, in 1870, was the first woman to hold the office of city physician in this or any other American city), Clay was a rising figure in local and state politics.

The uproar began in the winter of 1887, when Clay sued his wife's brother-in-law for alienation of affection. For weeks, the most intimate details of the family's personal affairs were splashed across the pages of the city's newspapers, often in verbatim testimony.

Defeated in his suit, emerging with the reputation of a hard-drinking, brutal, habitual gambler, the prosecutor then went through a thoroughly messy divorce from the doctor. On top of that came Smith's allegations that Clay solicited bribes, was in cahoots with certain saloon interests, and hindered the work of the police department. The trial dragged both men's professional standing through the mud, and the headlines of May 3, 1888, tell the outcome: "SAM CLAY BOUNCED." An order has come from Governor Cyrus Luce, removing the prosecutor from office. The press and the public have followed the whole disgraceful sequence with a relish that the sleaziest supermarket tabloids of 1988 would envy.

The scandals that will capture the public's attention in 1987-88 — Gary Hart, Edwin Meese, Iranscam, and the Pentagon contractors — are those on a national level. But a century earlier, some of the most infamous dirt is being shoveled right here in their own town.

Excitement has still not entirely died down over the sudden disappearance of Probate Judge Lyman Follet, who decamped last year after embezzling several thousand dollars of money entrusted to him. Sheriff L. K. Bishop still gets occasional reports that Follet has been spotted in one city or another, but none of these leads has ever panned out.

More recently, the mayoral election, held on August 3, 1888, turned into as disgraceful a contest as any in a long history of local political shenanigans. Republican Charles Belknap, a blunt-spoken Civil War hero turned wagon manufacturer, and Democrat Isaac Weston, a heavy-set bachelor "dandy" active in lumber and banking circles, battled through an acrimonious campaign.

On election night, accusations of cheating rang out from both sides, complete with accounts of midnight chases through dark streets after stolen ballot boxes. When the final count had Weston winning by only a nine-vote margin, Belknap filed a petition charging "error or fraud" in an attempt to void the result. Arguments flew hotly, both in and out of legal proceedings. Finally, on April 25, the Michigan Supreme Court affirmed Weston's victory, and the losing side is still furious.

(Only from our own twentieth-century vantage point can we appreciate the irony of knowing that the triumphant Weston is going to lose his fortune, political hopes, and everything else in the financial crash of 1893, dying broke and alone in New York a few years later. The defeated Belknap, meanwhile, will win election to Congress in November 1888 and live on to age 83, honored as one of his city's "grand old men," and still memorialized in 1988 by the park bearing his name and the bronze statue of him standing in it.)

No one knows it yet in May 1888, but city treasurer George Perry is about to begin embezzling city funds to help his party's congressional candidate, Democratic incumbent Melbourne Ford, win re-election in November. Ford will lose to Captain Belknap, but Perry's crime won't be uncovered for another three years. Such are the lax political ethics of the era that Perry will not only escape punishment, but he will be elected mayor in 1898 — and then go on to even bigger scandal with his connection to a crooked scheme involving bonds for a water pipeline to West Michigan.

So, if we're going to indulge in the nostalgia of a trip back a century in time, let's not extend it to oldtime Grand Rapids' municipal morals. A century hence, city politics will be considerably cleaner. In the 1987 election for mayor, victorious incumbent Gerald Helmholdt and his opponent, Edgar Kettle, might spar verbally, but modern methods of vote tallying will leave no margin for charges of election fraud. With luck, such abuses will be left to history.

There are other drawbacks to the "good old days."

If the past is a foreign country, the well-known traveler's adage might well apply: If you visit there, don't drink the water. The Grand, no different in the 1880s from any other river flowing through any other American city, is an open sewer as well as a drinking water supply. Tap water in summer comes out greenish and slimy, and anyone hoping to avoid typhoid must routinely boil it before drinking. Nevertheless, typhoid and other water-borne diseases still take their toll on human lives. The Hydraulic Company, a private concern which competes with the city in selling water to homes and businesses, uses natural springs as its source, but some of these are also becoming fouled.

Along the west city limits, where Garfield Avenue will someday run, lies the "big ditch," a noxious open sewer which drains waste from that side of town into the river below. All over the city are houses that lack indoor plumbing and where privies are often breeders of disease.

Only in the past year has the city Board of Health been reorganized and a professional health officer appointed. Dr. Hugo Lipinski, first

From left: Charles E. Belknap, Isaac M. Weston, Israel C. ("Bub") Smith.

8

to hold the position, is soon to be ousted on political grounds, having discovered too many embarrassing examples of unsanitary conditions and "stepped on too many toes." It will be 1912 before the city has a water filtration plant and 1930 before it will open its first sewage treatment plant.

Air pollution is another growing problem. With emission control laws still far in the future, unregulated coal and wood smoke from homes and industries need only a few years to turn the locally made cream-colored brick a dingy gray-brown. The problem is destined to grow worse before it gets better.

While the era of the 1880s, like most, has its pleasures for the wealthy few at the top of society's pyramid, the rising middle class often finds its aspirations at the mercy of an under-regulated and sometimes unscrupulous economic system. The working classes are materially less well off. Some of them form a substantial domestic

In this turn-of-the-century scene, looking southeast across the Grand River, the towers of the county courthouse and city hall are barely visible through the smoky haze.

servant workforce, and even modest households often employ at least one "hired girl" because so many poor, young women are available so cheaply. The working man's lot is characterized by long hours, low pay, and poor safety.

The newspapers routinely run stories of workers, some of them boys as young as fourteen, losing fingers or hands in factory accidents. If the victims survive, no certainty in this age of poor sanitation and limited medical care, they face a dismal future. If they're disabled, they are usually fired from their jobs, left only to their own meager resources and perhaps what little help charity can provide. Generally, they receive no medical aid from the company, no insurance, no unemployment benefits or workers' compensation from management or government. Local labor unions have almost no power, their influence broken after employers triumphed in a series of strikes in 1886.

We've already noted the absence of TV, stereos, VCRs, and movies. Among other modern technological advances you might miss if you had to stay here in the past are airplanes, automobiles, expressways, antibiotics, microwaves, refrigerators you don't have to load with ice every day, stoves you don't have to load with wood, and a whole host of other conveniences that later generations will take for granted.

In short, the past is like that old cliché about New York City: It's a nice place to visit, but we wouldn't want to live there. And yet, if you don't mind roughing it a little, the Grand Rapids of 1888 really has a lot to offer. As cities go in this era, it more than holds its own.

Grand Rapids can boast a remarkably good school system, whose graduates (admittedly a smaller percentage of the population than in the twentieth century) do well in the nation's finest colleges. The number of school buildings in town has nearly doubled in a decade, from twelve to twenty-three. The latest of these, the Madison Avenue primary at the corner of Madison and Fifth Avenue (Franklin Street), is now under construction and will open in the fall; young Jerry Ford will receive his elementary education here in about thirty years.

Public interest in Board of Education elections is unusually strong in Grand Rapids, perhaps because women who have school-age

Top: Public Library's reading room in the Ledyard Building.
Bottom: Central High School housed the collections of the Kent Scientific Institute, forerunner of the Public Museum.

children or own property are now actually allowed to vote in school elections and even run for seats on the board. This progressive innovation passed the state legislature in 1885 (thirty-five years before the Nineteenth Amendment to the United States Constitution granted suffrage to women), and this coming September, Mrs. Harriet Cook will become the first woman in the city to be elected to the Board of Education, or any other office, for that matter.

Despite the absence of electronic media, there is plenty to do for enjoyment. For a town its size, Grand Rapids has a good public library, soon to grow even larger when it moves into new quarters in the tower of the almost-completed City Hall. There's a small but very interesting museum operated by the Kent Scientific Institute, occupying rooms in the Central High School building. Though it can claim one of the finest natural history and archaeology collections in the Midwest, another fifteen years will pass before the museum moves into a home of its own.

All kinds of interests — from the social to the literary — find expression in the city's many clubs. Music societies for both men and women put on frequent concerts, some open to the public. A dozen or more bands and orchestras also exist, so that a performance is being held somewhere almost every day. A bandstand in Fulton Street Park, near downtown, is a popular spot for warm-weather concerts.

A note in the newspaper on May 3, 1888, tells us that the Bohemian band will be providing music for an excursion down to Grandville tomorrow on the *William H. Barrett*. The *Barrett* is about the last large steamboat on the Grand River, still regularly hauling passengers and some freight between here and Grand Haven. A few smaller, freight-hauling craft also continue to run, as do two or three little passenger steamers which have recently been making short runs upriver from the rapids. But river traffic in 1888 is just a fading echo of what it was before the railroad came in thirty years ago.

Besides riverboat trips, other pleasures that will not exist here in a hundred years are available to amuse Grand Rapids folk. These include horse races at the county fairground track; cricket matches held by a local club dedicated to that English sport; lacrosse games staged by a similar organization; and amateur baseball played at the fairgrounds. There's even talk of organizing a professional minor-league ball club here this year. Lawn tennis is popular among the well-to-do, but golf won't come to Grand Rapids for seven more years.

If all this isn't enough, there's no lack of quality entertainment to divert us. Let's check the newspapers again....

Hartman's Hall, at Fountain and Ionia, is the biggest auditorium in town, with two thousand regular seats and enough folding chairs to boost seating capacity to four thousand for special occasions. The hall opened last December with a spectacular recital put on by the Gage and Benedict dance school, and events have been taking place there almost constantly ever since. A huge Republican rally is scheduled for this week, and the Grand Rapids Oratorio Society is to present Handel's oratorio, *The Creation*, on May 13, with a hundred-voice choir and a thirty-piece orchestra. C. S. Hartman,

Grand Rapids and Saginaw fielded teams at this 1880s baseball game. Notice the "smoking section" sign in the grandstand.

the owner, also holds art exhibitions in some of the hall's rooms.

Theater-going is popular with the public here. Besides two or three smaller houses, there are three large facilities — Smith's Opera House, Redmond's Grand Opera House, and Powers' Grand Opera House.

Smith's is the town's vaudeville palace, where touring acts of comedy, music, acrobatics, and the like are the regular bill of fare; among "respectable" folk, this theater has a slightly shady reputation.

Redmond's Grand is the second-largest legitimate house. The *Eagle* notes that "Mattie Vickers, the pretty and piquant soubrette who has just closed a very successful engagement at the Windsor Theater in Chicago, will begin a week's engagement at Redmond's this evening in 'Jacquine.'"

And a city the size of Grand Rapids is not too far off the beaten track to enjoy the top-quality plays touring out of New York. At Powers' Grand Opera House, the jewel of local playhouses, Joseph Jefferson, probably the most beloved comic actor in America, will be appearing next week in his *Rip Van Winkle,* a perennial favorite for thirty years. Even more special, Edwin Booth and Lawrence Barrett, acclaimed as the world's greatest living tragedians, are performing *Othello* tonight at the Powers as part of their forty-week Shakespearean repertory tour, covering sixty-eight American cities. Local newspapers are reporting long lines at the box office, with some fans even sleeping there overnight to be sure of tickets.

These two great actors are said to make brief appearances at the whistle-stop towns along their route, stepping out of their private railroad car for some exercise, and giving fans who can't afford to attend their shows a look at the famous stars. The two silvery-haired gentlemen in tall silk hats promenade sedately up and down the platform, pretending not to notice the stir their presence causes.

Let's hope they have time to sample Grand Rapids' natural beauty before they move on. The Grand River valley is as pleasant a spot as any in the country, a place of green, rolling vistas of field and forest. Although most of the virgin woods that existed when the pioneers arrived have been cut down, residents now are coming to cherish the tall, stately trees which remain around the city.

Speaking of trees, here's a newspaper item reporting on a meeting of the "Hill Tree Planting Association" at "Smith's store on East Bridge Street." This so-called association, however, happens to be a well-meant hoax cooked up by a few local newspapermen not long ago. After a casual discussion of how much improvement shade trees would make in the appearance of the hill neighborhood east of downtown, the men decided to promote the idea by reporting meetings of the mythical organization in their papers, using the name of their lawyer friend, George W. Thompson, as its spokesman. Thompson's is the only name ever mentioned in the stories, and the meetings are always at an anonymous "Smith's" grocery store, barbershop, or whatever.

The funniest part is, a lot of citizens have actually gotten into the spirit of this movement to beautify the city's streets. They never seem quite able to find the meetings of the association, but they've been setting out trees on their own property all over the hill and urging their neighbors to do the same. The citizens of Grand Rapids don't know it yet, but in 1889 forty public-spirited gentlemen will form a real Kent County Tree Planting Association, looking to the bogus group as its model. Many streets of Grand Rapids future will grow leafy, green, and pleasant, thanks to this very "practical" joke.

Being a figurehead has not cost Thompson a dime to date, although he did have one close call. A woman representing the Union Benevolent Association, which runs a hospital in the neighborhood at Lyon and College, came to Thompson with a request to plant seventeen trees on the hospital's grounds. What could he do? The lawyer found himself going door to door for blocks around and he managed to collect enough donations to buy the trees.

But enough words. The whistle is blowing. Our train is pulling into Union Station, on the south side of downtown Grand Rapids. It's time to begin our tour.

Grand Rapids City Boundaries, Then and Now

Grand Rapids has grown dramatically in the past 100 years. As the gray shaded area on this map shows, the city of the 1880s covered an area of about eight square miles, bounded approximately by Sweet Street on the north, Fuller Avenue on the east, Hall Street on the south, and Garfield Avenue on the west. Today, the city covers 44.9 square miles and stretches in all directions to the boundary indicated by the map's bold black line. Much that was farmland a century ago is now densely populated urban area.

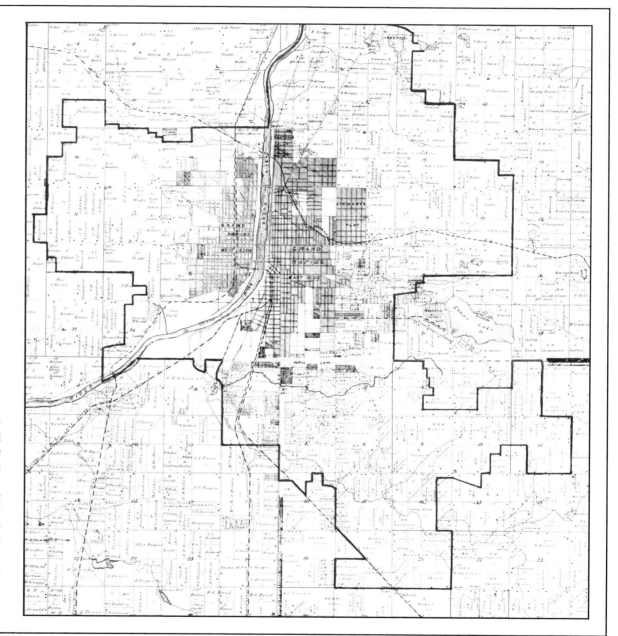

13

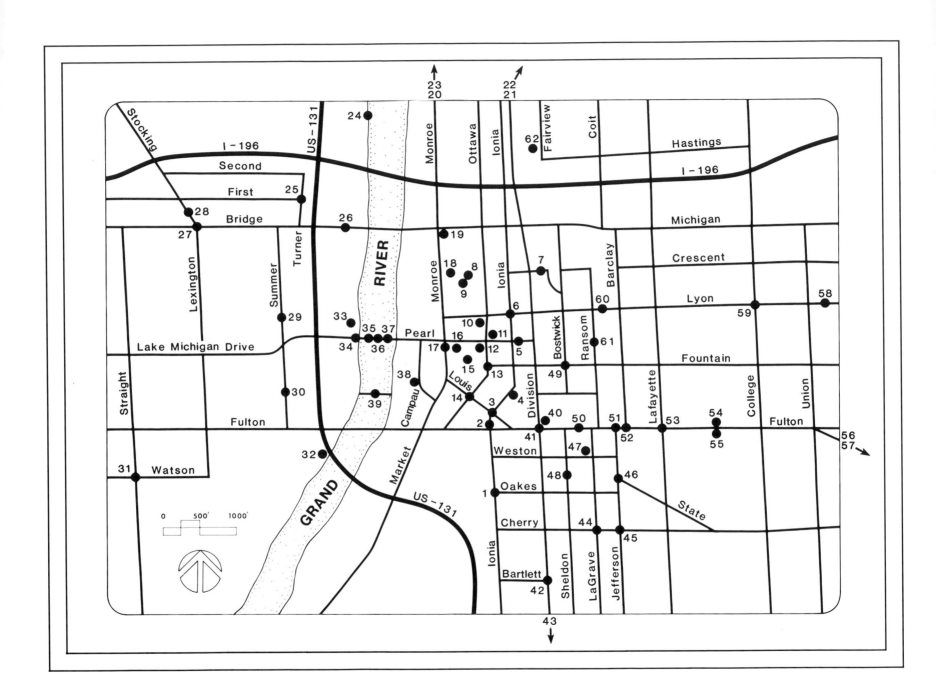

Tour Map and Guide to Then and Now Photographs

The numbered entries below correspond to the tour map and to the numbered photographs on the following pages.

1. Ionia Street from the Grand Rapids and Indiana Railroad offices (from Oakes Street)
2. South Ionia Street
3. O-Wash-Ta-Nong Boat Club (corner Ionia and Louis)
4. Monroe Street from the Morton House (Monroe Mall)
5. St. Mark's Episcopal Church
6. Grand Rapids Post Office and Federal Building (Grand Rapids Art Museum)
7. Entrance to Crescent Park
8. Crescent Street, looking east from Kent Street (Calder Plaza)
9. Engine house number four (Calder Plaza)
10. City Hall (corner Ottawa and Lyon)
11. Ledyard block
12. Houseman block (corner Ottawa and Pearl)
13. Peninsular Club
14. Ottawa, looking north from Louis
15. Widdicomb Building (Monroe Mall amphitheatre)
16. Sweet's Hotel (Amway Grand Plaza)
17. Canal Street, looking north from Monroe (Monroe, looking north from Pearl)
18. Bissell Carpet Sweeper factory (Hall of Justice)
19. Clarendon Hotel (Olds Manor)
20. Water works
21. Plainfield and Coit Avenue
22. Plainfield Avenue School
23. Michigan Soldiers' Home (Michigan Veterans' Facility)
24. Dam and east river bank below Sixth Street bridge
25. St. Mary's Catholic Church
26. West Bridge Street
27. West Bridge Street, looking east
28. Stocking Street
29. Summer Street from Allen
30. Phoenix Furniture Company
31. Straight Street School (neighborhood playground)
32. Grand River below Fulton Street bridge
33. West Side Power Canal (Ah-Nab-Awen Bicentennial Park)
34. Pearl Street bridge, looking east
35. Pearl Street bridge, looking west
36. Pearl Street bridge, looking north
37. Nelson, Matter Furniture factory, from Pearl Street bridge (George Welsh Civic Auditorium)
38. Kent County Jail (Oldtown Riverfront Building)
39. View from G.R.&I. bridge, looking south
40. Monroe, looking west from Division
41. Livingston Building (Junior Achievement building)
42. South Division Street School (Guiding Light Mission)
43. South Division, looking south from Sixth Avenue
44. LaGrave, looking north from Cherry
45. Cherry, looking east from Jefferson Avenue
46. Washington and State streets, looking east from Jefferson Avenue
47. Westminster Presbyterian Church
48. Ladies Literary Club
49. Bostwick, looking north from Fountain
50. Fulton Street Park (Veterans Memorial Park)
51. Jefferson Avenue, looking south from Fulton
52. East Fulton, looking east from Jefferson
53. Lafayette, looking south from Fulton
54. Harry Widdicomb residence (Peter A. Cook Administration Center of Davenport College)
55. George W. Gay residence
56. O-Wash-Ta-Nong Boat House (Reeds Lake docks)
57. Reeds Lake
58. Cable Car Power House (private residence)
59. Union Benevolent Association Home (Fountain School)
60. Lyon Street, looking east from Bostwick
61. Grand Rapids Central High School (Grand Rapids Junior College Learning Center)
62. Grand Rapids, looking west from bluff

Grand Rapids Then and Now
A Statistical Comparison

	1888	1988
Population (est.)	86,151	185,000
Area	8 sq. mi.	44.9 sq. mi.
Manufacturers	377	1,100
Churches	53	525 (est.)
Schools	23	92
Hotels	44	8
Motels	0	60
Railroad carriers	10	2
Passenger trains per day	45	2
Airlines	0	13
Passenger flights per day	0	90
Streets	143 mi.	556 mi.
Paved streets	8.6 mi.	524.9 mi.
Parks	6	49
Daily newspapers	4	1
Weekly newspapers	17	13
Public library holdings	25,000 vols.	702,258 vols.
Police stations	1	1
Police employees	71	295
Police equipment	2 wagons	110 motor units
Fire stations	8	13
Fire employees	85	281
Fire equipment	17 pieces	51 pieces

Grand Rapids Then and Now

Text by James VanVulpen

Contemporary photographs by Rex Larsen

Historical photographs from *Grand Rapids Illustrated,*
published in 1888

1

Welcome to Grand Rapids! It's a pleasant spring morning in 1888, and we have arrived by train at the city's Union Station, on Ionia Avenue at Oakes Street. As we leave the depot and turn north toward downtown, we get our first close-up view of the "Valley City." The block we're on now represents a neighborhood in transition. Once a mostly residential area known as "shantytown," its face has been changed by commercial development since the railroad came in about eighteen years ago. The Grand Rapids & Indiana line's building, put up in 1871, looms up on the left. Beyond it lies a block of wholesale grocery firms, and visible up at the corner of Ionia and Louis is the new Barnhart Building.

Welcome to Grand Rapids! We have just exited the U.S. 131 expressway on a fine spring day in 1988, approaching downtown from the south. It seems apt, considering how the automobile helped kill rail passenger traffic, that when the old railroad buildings were torn down in 1961, they were replaced by a freeway off-ramp. Much of the area once covered by track is now a vast parking lot. The old wholesale grocery buildings still stand, with extra stories added, but the Bishop Building, just ahead, blocks our view of the old Barnhart site. Having gone through a cycle of prosperity and decline during the past century, this district, now known as "Heartside," is currently moving toward a new revival.

2

Looking back south down Ionia from across Fulton Street, we can see the G.R. & I. Building facade and — just barely — the gable of Union Station beyond it. A little closer stand the Blodgett office building and the Putnam & Brooks candy factory. In the foreground, the Gunn Hardware block and the Hawkins & Perry grocery house are typical wholesale headquarters. Since the Civil War, Grand Rapids' wholesale trade has grown from two or three "jobbers" to about seventy firms. Most of them are in locations convenient to the rail lines, and they do a total business of over $12 million annually.

2

The rails are gone from this part of town, but the Gunn and Hawkins buildings, the latter now occupied by Copy-Right Printing, still stand almost as they appeared a century ago. Both buildings are examples of the refurbishing of historic structures that has marked Heartside's renewal in recent years. City officials hope that the trend will spread in years to come.

3

Grand Rapids has seen quite a construction boom during the past few years. One of the newer buildings is the Barnhart block, at the northwest corner of Ionia and Louis, completed in early 1887. The men of the O-Wash-Ta-Nong Boat Club, an athletic and social organization, have leased the building's upper floors for their downtown headquarters. The sporty young members are known to hold some lively entertainments here during the winter season. Later on our tour, we'll visit their summer clubhouse out at Reeds Lake.

The O-Wash-Ta-Nong Boat Club went bankrupt in 1892, and the Barnhart Building, which also housed many business office tenants over the years, was torn down in 1947. A city-owned parking ramp stood on the site for many years, but deterioration forced its removal just a year or two ago. This street-level lot may eventually see further development.

4

A block north, Ionia crosses Monroe Street, the city's main business thoroughfare. The Morton House, one of the best hotels in town, was built on this corner in 1873 as a plain, four-story block, but the owners added an ornate fifth floor just last year. Landlords are uncle and nephew, A. V. and J. Boyd Pantlind, who are said to set as good a table as you'll find in town. The Morton House is not cheap — $2.50 a day for a good room and three meals on the "American Plan" — but worth the price by all accounts. The hotel is also a favorite with exhibitors and buyers who trade here during the city's semi-annual furniture market.

Monroe became a pedestrian mall in 1980, its trees filling our view to the west. At right foreground is the recently renovated People's Building, which was built in 1916 on the site of an old row of stores. There is still a Morton House on the Ionia corner, but only the name is the same. The present building, put up in 1923, became the fourth hotel since 1835 to stand on this site. The hotel enjoyed a long era of popularity, rivaled only by the Pantlind, but the end of the furniture markets, coupled with Americans' changing travel habits, eventually spelled a decline in business. Converted to senior citizen housing in the 1970s, the Morton still stands as a downtown landmark.

4

5

Proceeding north on Ionia, we glance to our right as we cross Pearl Street. On Division Avenue, at the head of Pearl Street and surrounded by fine homes, stands St. Mark's Church, one of downtown's oldest buildings. The venerable structure was built of Grand River limestone in 1848, its twin towers added three years later. The stone eventually began deteriorating, so a stucco covering now conceals its original appearance.

5

With the advent of modern methods to preserve its original limestone walls, the church's stucco overcoat finally was removed in 1957. By that time, not a trace remained of the old residential neighborhood. Flanked by Grand Rapids Junior College at its rear and the telephone company building to its south, St. Mark's remains the oldest surviving structure in downtown Grand Rapids, radiating an air of mellow antiquity in contrast to the city's surrounding bustle.

6

Still proceeding north on Ionia, we pass the red brick Grand Rapids Post Office and Federal Building. Occupying the entire block bounded by Pearl, Lyon, Division, and Ionia, this was the town's first large government structure. The site, a "fine musical frog pond" in pioneer days, had to be extensively filled in before construction. Since its completion in 1879 after three years' work, the building has stood proudly amid the surrounding homes.

After space became so cramped that some local citizens sarcastically dubbed the old place "Noah's Ark," the federal government replaced the original brick structure with this much larger, gray stone building. President Theodore Roosevelt's daughter, Alice, laid its cornerstone in 1909. In the course of time, even this building was finally outgrown, first by the Postal Service, and then by the other federal offices. In 1981, after a long fund-raising campaign for remodeling, the Grand Rapids Art Museum moved in. The solid old Renaissance-style structure now looks forward to a proud future as one of the city's cultural landmarks.

6

Swinging around by Division Avenue, we pause at Crescent Street. To our east is the entrance to Crescent Park, a pleasant spot on the hill overlooking downtown. The property was donated to the city thirty years ago by Dr. George K. Johnson, who lived in the stone house (built in 1851 by Henry Williams, the city's first mayor) atop the bluff at right, and the Rev. Francis Cuming, whose mansion stands a half-block north. The park itself, however, wasn't really developed until recently. The ornate fountain, topped by a bronze nymph, and the stone steps were new in 1883.

7

An unfortunate by-product of the donors' generosity was the city's grading of Bostwick Avenue, which left their homes perched awkwardly on sand hills thirty feet above street level. The old Williams/Johnson house was torn down in 1890. Where its backyard once was, just beyond our angle of vision, stands Grand Rapids Junior College's Spectrum Theatre. Butterworth Hospital, built on the Cuming lot in 1925, has expanded over the years to occupy the entire block and more. Crescent Park's fountain lasted until 1949, and the steps have been repaved several times, but one thing hasn't changed. This is still one of the nicest spots in the city for a view of downtown.

8

Heading west on Crescent three blocks to Kent Street, we pass through a tree-lined residential neighborhood. This is soon to change, however. The block on our right as we face east has been chosen as the site of the new Kent County Courthouse. Groundbreaking is set for later this year. The courthouse will be finished in 1892, the same year that a handsome new Police Headquarters will rise across the street, on the northeast corner of Ottawa.

8

Not even the streets remain in 1988, let alone any sign that the area was once residential. Urban renewal in the mid-1960s removed the courthouse, police station, and other buildings. Where the intersection of Kent and Crescent was, we now find ourselves in the middle of Calder Plaza. Only the distant Crescent Park steps, framed by the 1967 NBD (formerly Union Bank) Building at right and the 1972 Frey Building at left, prove that we are in the same spot. Part of the sprawling Butterworth Hospital complex fills the rest of our view.

9

Turning to face northeast at the same corner of Crescent and Kent streets, we note one of the city's eight fire stations. Engine House number four in its present form dates from 1876. A much smaller original station, erected twenty years earlier on the north part of the lot, was incorporated into the enlarged structure. Number four serves primarily to protect the downtown area and neighborhoods just north of it. The gleaming brass engine, drawn by four mighty horses, is a thrilling sight to see charging up the street on its way to a blaze.

9

The city closed the old firehouse in 1938 after deciding that it was too run down to be worth repairing. Not only has the building been gone since 1940, but the entire block where it once stood simply vanished in the urban renewal of the 1960s. Today, nothing interferes with our view of the Probate Court Building on Ottawa, the Michigan State Office Building completed in 1976 at the Michigan Street corner, or the bluff beyond. The broad expanse of Calder Plaza surrounds us, and *La Grande Vitesse,* the big red stabile by Alexander Calder, is just out of the picture at the left. On the first weekend of each June, a half-million people throng this space for the city's annual arts festival, but on this spring morning all is quiet.

10

Heading back south on Ottawa, we pass a monument to years of civic effort. Of all the new buildings local citizens view with pride, none is quite so special as the City Hall. Almost finished, it promises an end to decades of wandering city government operations in modest rented quarters. Its cornerstone was laid in September of 1885, and gala ceremonies will dedicate it to the people of Grand Rapids almost exactly three years later. The handsome stone building was designed by Elijah E. Meyers of Detroit, and built by W. D. Richardson of Springfield, Illinois, at the astronomical cost of nearly $315,000.

10

Despite a fervent "Save Old City Hall" campaign, the building was doomed by urban renewal and demolished in 1969. Months of furious controversy climaxed with one ardent preservationist even chaining herself to the wrecking ball at the last minute, but without success. Though their effort was defeated, the loss galvanized local residents interested in keeping historic places from destruction. The eventual result was the creation of a civic unit, the Grand Rapids Historic Preservation Commission. In a belated nod to history, the tower site now holds a "time capsule," buried there beneath the shell of an Apollo spacecraft capsule as part of the national Bicentennial celebration in 1976.

11

Wealthy capitalist William B. Ledyard put up this building bearing his name in 1871 at the southwest corner of Pearl and Ottawa. One of the first large business blocks in town, it marked a new stage in the transition of the old Prospect Hill neighborhood from residential to commercial. In pioneer days, the hill rose sixty feet between Monroe and Ottawa and extended northward beyond Lyon Street. Although street gradings had already cut through the hill in 1857 and 1865, tons of earth still had to be dug away to make room for Ledyard's building, which, since its completion, has been home to the YMCA, the public library, and the Grand Rapids Business College, among other tenants.

One of the city's prime examples of urban rehabilitation, the Ledyard Building has been connected by its present owners to the older buildings that face the Monroe Mall behind it, forming one of the best-preserved landmark blocks in Grand Rapids. On the outside, this scene matches remarkably the appearance of its century-old counterpart, but the building's modern interior would dazzle its old-time tenants. Since the ten-million-dollar restoration was completed in 1987, stores, restaurants, and offices have begun to reoccupy the proud old structure. Its new life has demonstrated the business community's renewed confidence in the future of downtown Grand Rapids.

12

Julius Houseman was elected Grand Rapids' first Jewish mayor in 1872. A lumberman and former clothier as well as a Democratic politician, he erected this office building bearing his name in two stages. The four-story southern half, in the foreground at the Pearl and Ottawa corner, went up in 1883, and the five-story northern section was added three years later. To make room for his project, Houseman had all that remained of Prospect Hill's northeastern slope hauled away for fill dirt, marking a further stage in the hill's gradual disappearance. The massive block obscures our view of City Hall to the north and the Universalist Church immediately east. Down at the Ionia corner, at the eastern end of the block, stands the old Boyer house, a relic of times past, and just beyond that is the Federal Building.

Larger, more modern office structures had long since diminished the Houseman Building's prestige by the time it was torn down in 1966. The wreckers came just a little too early for the preservation movement which arose in the aftermath of the demolition of City Hall; a few more years, and the old place would have made a likely candidate for restoration. That was the good fortune of the Federal Square Building, on Pearl just to the right of the Ellis parking lot. Put up in 1892 and 1893, the building stands on the sites once occupied by the Boyer house and the Universalist Church.

13

A proud feature on the local social scene is the Peninsular Club, offering proof that a small midwestern town can enjoy the urban amenities. Some of Grand Rapids' leading gentlemen got together to organize a downtown men's club in 1881, and two years later they built this handsome clubhouse at the corner of Fountain and Ottawa. The grand ball that celebrated its opening in February of 1884 was the high point of the social season. With its rooms for cards, billiards, dining, and social receptions, the club's popularity is at an all-time high, with over three hundred resident and non-resident members.

13

The club had outgrown its quarters by the early twentieth century, but decided to remain on the site. The present building was opened in 1914, and a large addition on its east side was completed just sixty years later. With membership well above a thousand, the Peninsular Club still offers businessmen (and a few women, too, in recent years) the finest amenities a town club can provide. Dining and social events are still primary activities, but a well-equipped athletic department helps keep members in better shape than their nineteenth-century counterparts. In 1988, the indoor swimming pool and racquetball courts are more popular than the billiard room.

14

Two blocks south on Ottawa, we pause at Louis and look back northward. In the street, next to the three-story Hazeltine & Perkins wholesale drug company, are construction materials for the new Blodgett block going up off-camera at left. Further ahead, beyond the four-story White-Aldrich-Godfrey block, we see the old (1869) Aldrich block up at the Monroe Street jog, and adjacent to it at far left, the New Aldrich block (1884) on the corner of Fountain.

Hazeltine & Perkins moved out in 1911, though the building wasn't torn down for parking space until many years later. We now have an unobstructed view of the White-Aldrich-Godfrey Building. The Blodgett Building later became part of the huge Wurzburg department store building, which reached to Monroe and was demolished in 1973. But both Aldrich blocks are still standing, recently refurbished. The Michigan National Bank Building, erected in 1926, towers at right above the older structures.

14

15

Here's the Widdicomb Building, another of those new store and office buildings that the town boasts. William Widdicomb, who made his money in furniture, had the structure erected in 1886 on the site of the old wooden Rathbun House hotel, corner of Monroe and Waterloo. Down on the next corner, at Waterloo and Louis, is the Eagle (built in 1883 on the site of the 1834 pioneer inn of that name), Grand Rapids' leading temperance hotel.

An art deco-style Kresge's dimestore replaced the Widdicomb Building in 1935, a year after the Eagle Hotel was torn down. In 1978, the entire block was cut in two by the extension of Monroe Avenue (formerly Canal Street) through to Louis. Market (formerly Waterloo) was closed, as was old Monroe. Two years later, the Monroe Mall opened with great fanfare. Much of the celebration centered on this new amphitheatre at the mall's west end, which has since become the scene of many free downtown activities — ice skating in winter, concerts and dances in summer, to name only a few. Across the new Monroe Avenue stand the Campau Square Plaza Building (topped by the "Comerica" sign), the Square Center, and the PrimeBank (formerly Mutual Home) Building, all built during the 1980s.

16

One of the city's leading hostelries is Sweet's Hotel, right here on Campau Square. Martin Sweet, the richest man in town, built it in 1868, and has always kept it leased to reliable operators. Landlord N. C. Johnson has brought the place a fine reputation, making it the Morton House's only real rival as top hotel in Grand Rapids. Back in 1874, this whole building was jacked up four feet to match the new street grade, while business went on as usual with hardly a teacup broken. The Tower Clock Building, at left, was built in 1875.

Morton House proprietor J. Boyd Pantlind acquired Sweet's Hotel in 1896, after Martin Sweet went broke in the Panic of '93. In 1902, Pantlind changed the name to honor his uncle and mentor in the hotel business, A. V. Pantlind, and ten years later began construction of a new building. Erected in stages between 1912 and 1915, the Pantlind Hotel stood for decades as the number-one place to stay in downtown Grand Rapids before it fell on hard times. After being purchased by the Amway Corporation and closed for two years for complete refurbishing, the venerable hostelry reopened in 1981 as the Amway Grand Plaza. Behind the restored building rises the hotel's ultra-modern, twenty-nine-story glass tower, completed in 1983. The Tower Clock Building and its 1939 successor, a Woolworth dimestore, are both gone, replaced in the 1980s by the mirrored glass PrimeBank Building.

16

17

Looking up Canal Street from the Tower Clock Building, with Sweet's Hotel at left foreground, we see a commercial thoroughfare second only to Monroe Street. The blocks north from here were platted as the "Village of Kent" more than fifty years ago, but only since the Civil War have property owners made a significant investment in first-class brick buildings. As a matter of fact, they had to. The area's old wooden structures were claimed in a series of disastrous fires during the late 1860s and early 1870s.

Our vantage point has shifted to street level as we look up Monroe Avenue (the modern-day name of Canal Street), which has run through this site since 1978. North of Lyon Street (one block north of Pearl), as far as the eye can see, not a single structure remains from a century ago. The block on our immediate left gave way long ago to the Pantlind Hotel, today part of the Amway Grand Plaza. But on the east side of the street between Pearl and Lyon, every building shown in the 1888 picture still exists, some enlarged and all under new facades.

18

As we pass along Canal Street a block north of Lyon, if we could see over the stores on our left, we would have this view of the Bissell Carpet Sweeper factory — the largest of its kind in the world. Company founder Melville R. Bissell built the structure four years ago, after a disastrous fire wiped out the earlier plant he had built on the same site. The six-story office building went up beside it in 1885. Water power to drive the factory's machinery is supplied by the old East Side Power Canal, which was completed in 1842 and flows behind the buildings.

Since the stores fronting Canal Street (now Monroe Avenue) disappeared during urban renewal, the closest we can come to our original vantage point is from the western edge of Vandenberg Center, just west of the County Building. The city filled in the east side canal around 1928, after factories alongside it had switched to steam or electric power. The Bissell plant was torn down in 1959, following the company's move to a facility in suburban Walker. After being used for years as a parking lot, the land became the site of the south end of the Hall of Justice in 1966 and the northern portion of the Grand Center parking ramp in 1980.

19

The Clarendon Hotel, standing at the northwest corner of Canal and Bridge streets, was opened in 1878 as the Rasch Hotel. Renamed two years later by Edward Killean, its new proprietor, the Clarendon is popular with small-time traveling salesmen, lumberjacks, and other guests who find Sweet's or the Morton House a bit too rich. Just west of the hotel is the Valley City Milling Company's flour mill, built on the East Side Power Canal in 1867.

19

When the Valley City mill burned down in 1923, it and the old Clarendon building were replaced by the large and elegant Rowe Hotel. After operating for nearly forty years as a close competitor to the Morton House and the Pantlind, the Rowe, like the Morton in the following decade, closed its doors to the hotel trade in 1961. Conversion to senior citizen housing soon followed. Now named the Olds Manor, the building is home to several hundred residents. The 1962-vintage post office building adjoins it on the north and west.

20

Continuing north on Canal Street, we come to a jog at Coldbrook, where the city water works pumping station is located. Built in 1874, after extensive downtown fires pointed up the need for a municipal water supply, the pumping station can draw from Coldbrook and Carrier creeks and the Grand River. Engineers now warn that the creeks are growing too polluted to be used much longer, but several efforts to raise funds for improvements have been turned down by the voters. This coming August, however, citizens will approve a $168,000 bond issue to finance a switch to filtered river water, the construction of a new boiler house, and the replacement of the old wooden pipe with cast iron as the city's water mains are extended to fifty-nine miles, more than double their present length.

20

After several expansions over the past century, a few parts of the old water works' walls still exist inside the modern building which completely surrounds them. The plant can pump up to eighty-three million gallons per day, though average use is only about half that. Lake Michigan has been the main source of supply since 1940, and the water now gets thoroughly purified. In 1945, Grand Rapids became the first city in the nation to fluoridate its drinking water to prevent dental decay. Today, just as a hundred years ago, the city continues its efforts to deliver a clean, plentiful water supply to satisfy an ever-growing demand.

21

The fork at Plainfield and Coit Avenue marks the heart of a growing neighborhood known simply as the "north end." The city limit ends at Sweet Street, just a quarter-mile away, and most of what lies beyond is open country. Past the city line, Plainfield becomes a gravel toll road that runs nine miles north to the bridge crossing the north bend of the Grand River. Here at the intersection, Mrs. Eliza Page, one of the city's few independent businesswomen, owns and operates this drugstore, living upstairs with her family.

21

Urban growth has pushed the city limits two and a half miles northward during the past century, leaving the "north end" area well inside. Grown into a thriving business district, the neighborhood was renamed "Creston" in 1907 following a contest sponsored by its merchants. The old Page block eventually became a branch of Kent State Bank, which replaced the original building with the present one around 1925. In recent years, the building has housed the Creston branch of the Grand Rapids Public Library.

22

A short distance north of the fork lies the Plainfield Avenue School. The original six-room building was erected in 1884, but the north end's rapid growth forced a four-room addition just a couple of years later. The school's capacity is now five hundred students. The three little girls standing beside the building could tell you that Miss Doyle, the principal, runs a strict, no-nonsense regime, with a strong emphasis on the educational basics.

The encroachment of commercial development, a deteriorating building, and cost-cutting measures dictated by the Great Depression led to the closing of Plainfield School in 1933 and the distribution of its pupils among the Eastern, East Leonard, and Palmer schools. The present building was put up on the site in 1938 as an A & P food store and later was occupied for years by an Eberhard's market. More recent tenants have included an insurance office and a Baptist mission. For the past few years, the structure has been the laboratory of Optical Supply, Inc.

23

On the Canal Street gravel road, two miles north of the city limits, stands the massive Michigan Soldiers' Home. Built by the state to house a growing population of aging and infirm Civil War veterans, it was occupied on the first day on 1887. Landscaping hasn't yet been completed, and already an increase in applications beyond the building's capacity of 450 is pressing the legislature to erect an addition dormitory and a hospital on the grounds. At a dock on the Grand River nearby, we can catch a ride back into town on a small kerosene-powered steamboat, the *Grand Island,* which makes regular trips between the home and the Sixth Street bridge.

Now known as the Michigan Veterans' Facility, the institution celebrated its centennial in 1986. "Old Main," as the original structure became known, didn't quite survive to see the day. Torn down in 1973, it was replaced by the modern McLeish Building, a 343-bed nursing-care facility, which is the center of a complex serving over 730 veterans. The new unit also houses administrative offices, dietary and dining facilities, a special section for about fifty women, and well-equipped occupational, physical, and recreational therapy departments. The only surviving nineteenth-century relic on the grounds is the 1893-vintage fountain, recently restored.

24

We've left the riverboat at the Sixth Street bridge, crossed to the west side, and come down the bank two blocks to look back north and eastward. The east end of the bridge, built just two years ago, shows clearly at left, as does Charles C. Comstock's four-story building, standing between the bridge and Canal Street. An earlier wooden dam that stretched across the river was replaced by this one in 1866, when William T. Powers began constructing the West Side Power Canal. Note the chute at the dam's center, designed to allow logs to float freely downriver to the sawmills. The top of that sandy eastern bluff is becoming built up with houses, and a flight of wooden steps has been installed to afford workers who live there faster access to the factories below.

24

We can't stand at exactly the same 1888 vantage point, because the Grand River fish ladder covers that original spot today. The western half of the old dam was rebuilt in concrete after a washout around 1916, and the eastern half was replaced four years later. Old Sixth Street bridge, thanks to the efforts of local preservationists, received landmark status, got a complete overhaul, and was dedicated in 1981. The Comstock Building, with a recent addition, also survives. Concrete steps along the eastern hillside have been allowed to decay and are hidden by the growth of trees and brush which now covers the once-bare slopes.

25

At the northwest corner of Turner and First streets stands St. Mary's Roman Catholic Church. A large portion of the west side's early settlers were German immigrants, and the parish was created in 1856 for those of the Catholic faith, offering sermons in their native language. The present building was consecrated in 1874, during the pastorate of Father John G. Ehrenstrasser, but its spire, designed by noted Grand Rapids architect William Robinson, wasn't added until ten years later. Dutch and Polish Catholics also attended here for many years, but have more recently formed parishes of their own.

25

St. Mary's still stands today, looking not much different than it did a hundred years ago, although the U.S. 131 expressway embankment now faces it across the street. A new vestibule, on either side of the spire, built by Father John J. Riess in the 1920s, has enlarged the church's capacity, and the parish school beside the church, built in 1893, was extensively remodeled in 1958. Widespread anti-German sentiment during World War I hastened the end of German-language services, but gradual assimilation of the immigrants and their descendants probably would have had the same effect eventually.

26

Bridge Street, here seen westward from Front, is the west side's main business thoroughfare, built up in brick after a huge fire in 1875 wiped out sixty-two of the wooden buildings which lined it before. Now the area is practically a small city in itself — you can find just about anything you want here without crossing the river. There are dry goods shops, groceries, blacksmiths, drugstores (two of them at this corner), railway depots, restaurants, even the Fifth National Bank, specially organized by west-side men two years ago. A few people even talk only half jokingly about someday seceding to form a separate "City of West Grand Rapids."

Secession sentiment reached serious height after a great flood in 1904 inundated the west side, the result, according to its citizens, of neglect by city leaders. Floodwall construction and other attentions by the city gradually quieted the movement, and West Grand Rapids never came to be. A major change in the streetscape came when the U.S. 131 expressway went through in 1962. The stretch between the highway and the river stands blocked until November 1988 for construction of a new Bridge Street bridge, the sixth span since 1845 to cross the river at this point.

27

At its other end, looking east from Stocking, the West Bridge Street business district begins to grow partly residential. Charles Pettersch owns the grocery store and saloon at left foreground and lives above it with his family. Though the neighborhood is predominantly German, many Poles and Swedes have also moved in, adding to the mixed ethnic flavor.

Named Stockbridge in a contest in 1982, the neighborhood is still one that especially reflects Grand Rapids' richly varied ethnic heritage. Within a half-mile radius of this spot live people whose origins range from Hispanic to Lithuanian, and Chippewa to Vietnamese, among many, many others. The old Pettersch place was a laundromat before its demolition a few years ago, but other buildings in the area have been or soon will be renovated. Just out of view at our left is Little Mexico, one of the city's most popular Mexican restaurants, a former sausage factory restored by entrepreneur Martin Morales.

28

Stocking Street runs northwest from Bridge. Billius Stocking and his brother laid out the road to their land claim without using a compass, chopping through the underbrush as they went. More than fifty years later, "Uncle Billy" still lives in his original house, up at the far end of this mostly residential street. To our right, at the corner of First Street, is an enterprise that the old pioneer probably never imagined when he settled here — the Eagle Brewery, established in 1876 by Jacob Veit and Paul Rathman. One of eight large breweries in Grand Rapids, it turns out a popular lager beer.

28

The I-196 expressway, a considerably more complicated feat of engineering than the Stockings' old trail, crosses Stocking Avenue a few blocks north. Another memorial to the Stocking name is the elementary school which has stood since 1921 on the site of the pioneer house. More businesses than homes line the street today. The last brewing companies have, for good or ill, vanished from Grand Rapids. On the other hand, places like the Pizza Queen abound in every neighborhood — and you couldn't buy a pizza anywhere in town a hundred years ago.

29

The west-side land south of Bridge Street was developed largely by Deacon James Converse, a Boston capitalist. In 1850, he bought what was once an Ottawa cornfield and had his agents grade, plat, and plant the streets with rows of handsome trees. Summer Street, looking north from Allen toward Bridge, is a typical middle-class, residential, west-side street. Many of the prominent German families in town have addresses in this neighborhood.

29

Some of the old houses still line the avenue, though most of the trees are gone. More of a working class neighborhood now, with fewer private homes and more apartments, the area still retains a solid, family atmosphere.

Grand Rapids enjoys a growing reputation as a furniture-manufacturing center, and one of the local industry's best-known names is the Phoenix Furniture Company, whose plant stands at the corner of West Fulton and Summer streets. The original building, completed in 1873, has grown with additions in 1875, 1880, and 1883. Every year, the factory turns out $700,000 worth of chamber suites, folding beds, bookcases, dining tables, and heavy office furniture. Deacon Converse is the company's president, but probably the best known of Phoenix's 550 employees is David W. Kendall, a designer of national reputation.

The Phoenix name survived until 1920, when the company merged with another firm to become the Robert W. Irwin Furniture Company. (David Kendall's name lives on today through the Kendall College of Art and Design, founded in 1928 by his widow, Helen.) The Irwin years saw further additions to the original Phoenix plant, and after World War II, three successive companies continued to produce furniture there. The last of these was Stow & Davis, now owned by Steelcase, Inc., and operating out of a newly built plant in Kentwood. In 1987, Steelcase donated the old plant to Grand Valley State University to be used for west bank campus development. Preservationists still hope the building might somehow be saved as a monument to the boom years of the Grand Rapids furniture industry.

31

These six boys lounging on its lawn might be surprised to learn that only half a century ago, the site of Straight Street School was the center of the southernmost of two Ottawa Indian villages near the rapids. Few Indians remained in the area when this modern schoolhouse was built in 1885 at the southeast corner of Straight and Watson streets. Serving elementary students in the city's southwestern corner, it holds 363 children, plus an additional eighty who attend classes in an old wooden building at the rear.

The old school educated generations of west siders (including a number of Native Americans) until the ravages of age forced its demolition in the 1960s. Its site, now a small neighborhood park, is still a magnet for children. The youngsters of 1888 would be delighted by the modern playground equipment, but they'd probably be shocked by a passing jogger. The idea of grown men (much less women!) running in the streets for fitness and pleasure would likely seem fantastic to them.

32

This Grand River scene, looking northeast from a grassy spot on the west bank below downtown, shows the east end of the new (1884) Fulton Street bridge at the extreme left. The east river bank opposite us is actually part of a row of islands that were connected to the mainland as the channel was gradually filled in. Rising above the skyline are the smokestack of the new Edison Light and Fuel Company's power plant, the spire of Fountain Street Baptist Church, and on the distant hill beyond, the Central High School.

The same view today looks out from beneath the S-curve of the U.S. 131 expressway. Only a scrap of muddy riverbank remains, below a high floodwall which protects the west side from high water. On the opposite bank, Charley's Crab, a popular seafood restaurant, overlooks the water. A few hundred feet upstream, we see the eastern spans of the Dean Memorial Bridge, which has carried Fulton Street traffic across the Grand River since 1927.

32

33

Following Front Street upstream along the riverbank, we get a close look at the West Side Power Canal. This view faces northward from a footbridge a little north of Pearl Street. When William T. Powers built this canal, completed in 1869, he dredged up earth from the riverbed to create a new bank, rather than digging through dry land as the builders of the east side canal had done. Powers saved a lot of money that way, but his action narrowed the Grand considerably where it flows through downtown.

Not a trace remains of the old canal today. Its usefulness as a power source gone, it was finally filled in during the 1960s. Ah-Nab-Awen Bicentennial Park, which forms a kind of riverfront "yard" for the Gerald R. Ford Presidential Museum, stands almost completely on land that was once under water. Out on the river, just beyond the interurban bridge that leads into the park, are the arches of the old Bridge Street bridge, being demolished this spring of 1988.

33

34

To cross back to the east side, we'll take the new Pearl Street bridge. In June of 1883, a huge runaway log jam roared down the river in the downtown area, so badly damaging Pearl Street's original (1858) covered wooden span and a similar one at Bridge Street that both had to be replaced. The bridge at Pearl Street was built two years ago, at a cost of $41,000, by the Massillon Bridge Company, an Ohio firm specializing in this steel truss design. Note the double set of horsecar tracks running down the length of the bridge.

The Massillon bridge was replaced in 1922 by a modern concrete span, which was widened to its present size some sixty years later. The Pearl Street exit from U.S. 131 on the west side makes this one of the main gateways to downtown. Ahead of us on the east bank at left stands the Amway Grand Plaza Hotel tower. To the right is the restored Forslund Building, which houses the Carl Forslund furniture showrooms at street level and twenty luxury condominium units on its upper floors.

35

At the center of Pearl Street bridge, we pause for a panoramic view northward along the west bank. Lining the canal, from left, are the Powers & Walker Casket Company, Blackmore Manufacturing, and F. L. Furbish's furniture shop. Across Front Street a little further north are Daniel Sullivan's boiler works and Joseph Jackoboice's West Side Iron Works, the latter housed in what used to be the German-American schoolhouse. Beside the iron works is the tent of a traveling minstrel show that will be moving on in a day or two. Just south of Bridge Street is Voigt & Herpolsheimer's Star Mill, which produces a popular brand of flour. At far right is the Weirich block, on Bridge Street.

The mills and factories are long gone from the west bank. In their places stand the Gerald R. Ford Presidential Museum and Ah-Nab-Awen Bicentennial Park. The footbridge leading to the park was originally built in 1914 for interurban trolleycars. The old schoolhouse/iron works building north of the museum was slated to be preserved as an historic landmark, but a fire set by arsonists destroyed it in 1981. The white water in the foreground is caused by a low dam, one of four placed at intervals in the river back in 1927 to help maintain water levels. The Weirich block survives, home of Sullivan's Furniture and Carpet Store.

Turning due north, we see the new iron Bridge Street bridge a few blocks upriver. In 1884, just after the old bridge had been taken down for replacement, an item in the *Daily Eagle* noted that people crossing on Pearl could now look northward and "see a dam site better." Visible along the east bank south of the bridge are the Bissell Carpet Sweeper factory and, at extreme right, the five-story Butterworth & Lowe machine shop.

36

Once again, another Bridge Street bridge is being removed and replaced, but now the interurban bridge blocks our view. Further upstream we can spot the two I-196 bridges spanning the river at different levels. On the east bank, we now get a clear view of the post office and, further south, the city's Hall of Justice.

37

Now facing northeast from the Pearl Street bridge, we see the Butterworth & Lowe foundry and machine shop at left, and the Nelson, Matter furniture factory, built in 1873, on the right. The former originated with a small iron works on the site in 1845. The latter, dating back to 1855 under different owners, is the oldest large-scale furniture manufacturer in town. Behind the factory, we see the walls going up for Nelson, Matter's new seven-story office building and warehouse. Built to replace an older building which was destroyed in November 1887 in a spectacular blaze, it will be the largest structure of its kind in the state outside Detroit.

When Nelson, Matter moved out in 1914, part of the old factory became a station for the interurban trolleys running to Kalamazoo, and the bridge was built to carry their tracks across the river. After the interurban went broke in 1926, furniture magnate Gus Hendricks planned to close Lyon Street and build a huge skyscraper "Furniture Temple," of which his Fine Arts Building (at right) would be part. The Depression ruined his plans, however, and in 1932 the city erected its Civic Auditorium on the site. Now renamed for George W. Welsh (1883-1974), the city manager who championed its construction, the auditorium is part of the Grand Center complex.

38

Reaching the east bank, a turn south on Campau Street to the corner of Louis brings us to the Kent County jail, which has stood here since 1871, on what was originally an island in the Grand River before the east channel was filled. Erected at a cost of nearly $50,000, the brick and stone structure proved to be no match for those escape-minded prisoners who got away by digging through the walls. To avoid any further embarrassment, officials had the jail's inside walls sheathed with heavy boiler iron in 1884. The sheriff's office and living quarters are in the building, and there's a yard where convicts get their exercise by breaking stone, which the county sells for construction material.

OLDTOWN
RIVERFRONT
BUILDING
248 LOUIS CAMPAU
PROMENADE

When it was first built, the jail stood close to the river's edge, but later filling further extended the shoreline. The Citizens' Telephone Company, a local competitor of the Bell system, built its headquarters on the east bank between the jail and the river in 1903 and a year later originated the first automatic dial phone service in any large American city. When the decrepit and overcrowded old jail was finally torn down in 1958, its site became this parking lot. In 1973, the old phone building, long used for storage after Citizens' and Bell merged in the 1920s, was completely renovated to become the Oldtown Riverfront Building. This office project proved so successful that owners doubled its size with an addition in the early '80s.

39

The Grand Rapids & Indiana Railroad trestle crosses the river just south of the jail. Walking out to the middle of it, we look southwest to the Fulton Street bridge. The first link between East and West Fulton streets, the bridge has given the west side a tremendous boost since opening over two years ago. New business blocks like those at extreme right are going up along the street, and new factories like Colby, Craig & Company's wagon works are being built beside the riverbank. The railroad bridge we're standing on is fairly new, too, a replacement for one swept away by the great logjam of '83.

The 1885 iron Fulton Street span is gone, and the concrete Dean Memorial Bridge has stretched across the river since 1927. The old railroad bridge gave way to this replacement in 1903. Recently refurbished as a footbridge, it links Grand Valley State University's new $28 million L. V. Eberhard Center with development on the east side. Both bridge and building were dedicated with festive ceremonies on April 29, 1988. Congressman Paul Henry declared that "fifty years from now, when Grand Rapids celebrates its centennial, this day and this building will be recalled as one of the important milestones in our community's history."

40

Before turning to the south and east sides, we take one last look back at downtown from its eastern edge, down Monroe Street from Division. The upper end of Monroe developed into a business district in the mid-1870s. The Peck brothers opened their drugstore in 1876 in the wedge-shaped corner building, erected the year before. Along with the row extending west, the building is owned by wealthy capitalist Amos Rathbone. The building at right on the northeast corner of Division was built by real estate dealer John C. Wenham in 1878, and the large Porter block, not quite visible across Monroe on the left, went up in 1877.

Peck's Drugs continued operating under that name until Revco bought out the company in 1967. Just a few weeks ago, the Revco store moved into new quarters further down Monroe Mall, ending 112 years of continuous drugstore operation at this corner. The building that Revco vacated is the original 1875 structure, under an aluminum skin added during the early 1960s in an attempt to "modernize" it. The Wenham block also still stands, recently restored to like-new condition. The Porter block gave way in 1948 to Herpolsheimer's department store, the same structure that now houses the City Centre shopping mall.

41

On the southeast corner of Division and Fulton, workers are putting the finishing touches on the almost-completed Livingston Building, the city's first six-story "skyscraper." The brand new building transforms the spot where the old wooden 1838 Lovell Moore house, the first home built south of Fulton, stood until only a few years ago. (A pioneer humorist nicknamed the old place the "House of the Apostolic Succession," because it "reached so far back" on its lot.) The new building will be used as a residential hotel, with the Grand Rapids Savings Bank occupying the corner storefront. Its owners anticipate a bright future.

The Livingston went up in flames on the night of April 1, 1924, in one of the worst conflagrations Grand Rapids ever saw. Eight people died, either in the fire or jumping from upper windows. Until they were leveled four years later, the burned-out walls stood on the corner as a grim reminder of the tragedy. During the next two decades, while the site was used for parking, the hotel's old floor tiles could still be seen. In 1949, Davenport Institute (now Davenport College of Business) erected the present building and used it until outgrowing it in the mid-1960s. Today it is the home of Junior Achievement.

42

Proceeding southward, we pass South Division Street School, at the northwest corner of Division and Bartlett. With fourteen rooms and a capacity of seven hundred students, it's the biggest elementary building in town, but the large number of children in the neighborhood obviously justifies the city's $32,000 investment. Completed in 1884 on the site of two earlier wooden structures, this school is the pride of the near south side.

Changing urban patterns in the twentieth century gradually shifted the school-age population to other parts of town. The old building's days as a school had long since ended, and its crumbling rooms were used only for storage before it was torn down in 1948. In 1962, the Michigan Unemployment Security Commission erected the present building, and occupied it until 1985. Still serving the people of the Heartside neighborhood, it now houses the Guiding Light Mission.

43

The southern side of town is Grand Rapids' most rapidly growing area. Not many years ago, this part of South Division Street, here looking north from Sixth, was known simply as the old Antoine Campau farm, settled in 1845 by the brother of Grand Rapids' founder. Since the horsecar tracks were extended in 1873 to the county fairgrounds, which stand just outside the city limits at Hall Street, homes and businesses have sprung up all along Division and surrounding streets. This coming season, over a hundred new buildings are expected to rise in the Hall-Division vicinity, only a half-mile south of here.

43

Antoine Campau's name still survives. His grandson, philanthropist Martin A. Ryerson, gave a part of the old farm to the city for Campau Park in 1899, and Sixth is now called Antoine Street. After years as a predominantly Italian neighborhood, the area began changing after World War II, as thousands of new black residents began settling here. The transition was not without problems, and South Division was the scene of riots in the late 1960s. The park became the site of Campau Commons, Grand Rapids' first public housing project. The forty-unit project, erected at a cost of $600,000, opened in 1969. In recent years, the street has begun a comeback, as the location of several growing minority-owned businesses.

44

Heading back toward the center of town, we turn east on Cherry Street, passing through a residential neighborhood whose prestige is second only to the "hill district." A glance northward on LaGrave reveals a row of genteel, well-to-do homes. That of clothing-store owner Joseph Houseman is faintly visible up on Fulton Street. The horsecar line that runs on Cherry connects via Wealthy Street to the "dummy line," a steam railway going out to the resorts at Reeds Lake.

44

Very few residences line the street in 1988, and no one would call those that remain "well-to-do." Yet, in the area of religion, a certain element of prestige does linger in the neighborhood. The LaGrave Avenue Christian Reformed Church, whose spire rises on our left, is one of the most respected in its denomination. Westminster Presbyterian, which we'll see later, continues to thrive up the street. And First (Park) Congregational, which removed the old Houseman home for parking in 1985, recently celebrated its 150th birthday.

45

The further east we go on Cherry, the more elegant become the homes. If we were to proceed on past Madison, we'd see several large estates belonging to the town's wealthier families. Lumber baron Delos A. Blodgett, for example, lived in the third house at right until quite recently, but he's bought an even bigger mansion down the street and turned his old place over to his daughter, Susan, and her new husband, Edward Lowe, as one of their wedding presents. But we'll see other fine homes later. Let's turn north on Jefferson for a few more sights.

45

In a hundred years, downtown has expanded to take in the former residential neighborhood. St. Mary's Hospital, at right, started back in 1893 when members of the McNamara family donated their big house around the corner of Cherry and Lafayette to the bishop of the Catholic diocese for hospital use. The institution has gradually expanded to occupy the whole block, along with its neighbor, the Mary Free Bed Hospital and Rehabilitation Center, which faces Wealthy Street.

46

Another glance eastward from Jefferson, down Washington and State streets, proves that we're still in an elegant neighborhood. Sixty years ago, State was just an Indian trail; later, it took its name from being part of the old state road to Kalamazoo. Now, lumberman T. Stewart White lives in the big house at center with his wife and five sons. White's extensive logging operations have made him rich, and he also is half-owner of the company that floats all cut logs downriver between Grand Rapids and Grand Haven, sorting and delivering them to the sawmills there. His oldest son, Stewart, is gaining local fame as one of the best rifle shots in Kent County.

46

Crack shot Stewart Edward White (1873-1946) became a best-selling author in the early 1900s with his action-packed novels of the Michigan lumber era and the "Wild West." One of his brothers, Gilbert White (1876-1939), a successful artist, lived much of his life in France. Another, Roderick (1890-1945), was a noted concert violinist. This talented clan's old homestead was torn down in 1918, and its site is now the parking lot for a medical building. Other homes on the block also came down, and by the mid-1950s, State Street had become almost completely commercial. In the little triangular park before us stands the Calkins Law Office, Grand Rapids' oldest surviving pioneer building, put up in 1836 and moved here and restored in 1976 as part of the Bicentennial celebration.

47

Westminster Presbyterian Church, at the southeast corner of LaGrave and Island streets, was the first east-side congregation of its denomination. Organized in 1861 and first located in a small building on North Division, where the post office stands today, the group built church foundations and a chapel on this site in 1875. The main structure went up in 1885 and was occupied on October 1 of that year. Fashionable homes surround the church. The one down on the Jefferson corner is the D. Darwin Hughes residence, built in 1871.

Island Street is now Weston. The old Hughes house, which served for many years as an annex of the Grand Rapids Public Museum, was torn down in the late 1930s. Westminster, however, continues to thrive. Additions over the years have expanded its area to cover most of the block. And although its original demographics have changed, Westminster, like other downtown churches — Fountain Street, Park Congregational, St. Mark's Episcopal, First United Methodist, Immanuel Lutheran, LaGrave Avenue Christian Reformed, and St. Andrew's Cathedral, among them — has chosen to stay at the city's heart and carry on a metropolitan ministry.

48

One of the newest landmarks on the local cultural scene is the Ladies Literary Club on Sheldon Avenue. Over four hundred of the town's most socially prominent women belong to this association dedicated to their intellectual advancement. The outgrowth of a small history class of young women in 1869, the club officially organized in 1872 for study of history, art, science, and literature. Its growing popularity led to the erection of this clubhouse, the first of its kind in America. The cornerstone was laid July 30, 1887, and the handsome building, designed by William G. Robinson, opened its doors this past New Year's Day.

48

Any of its founders would have no difficulty recognizing their clubhouse today. The building underwent a major remodeling and enlargement in 1930, and another renovation in time for its centennial in 1987, but its white brick, stone, and terra cotta facade remains virtually unchanged. Its auditorium, bigger now than originally, still boasts superb acoustics, and a splendid stained glass window, designed by Louis Comfort Tiffany in 1915, continues to preside over the library. The club has been the scene of countless fascinating programs over the years, many in recent times open to the general public as well as members. Still a beacon of culture in Grand Rapids, the "Ladies Lit" is advancing zestfully into its second century.

49

Let's begin our buggy ride out to Reeds Lake with a look at the residential neighborhood just east of downtown. We're on Bostwick Avenue, north of Fountain Street, and that shadowy outline almost hidden by the trees at right is the tower of Second Reformed Church. This is not a remarkable street, except for one thing — those two ancient elm trees in the middle of the road a little beyond the Lyon intersection. An estimated three hundred years old, the trees were a hot topic of controversy not long ago when the city's Common Council announced plans to cut them down. Scores of citizens protested, and local lawyer/poet E. D. G. Holden sprang to the elms' defense in verse. The council backed down, and it looks like the trees are to be spared.

If we peek around the "Do Not Enter" sign, we'll see that the trees are gone. So, in fact is everything else in sight from a hundred years ago. But the Bostwick elms, protected by preservationists, lived on until old age took them in 1953. A section of one's trunk, its rings marked with dates, is on permanent exhibit at the Grand Rapids Public Museum. The building at left was originally built in the 1920s as the George A. Davis Vocational and Technical High School — "Davis Tech" to everyone — but since 1945 it's been the Grand Rapids Junior College main building. The JC parking ramp across the street came much later, in 1975.

50

Seen from its southeast corner, Fulton Street Park looks handsome with the soft green haze of spring buds on its trees. Once known as the "Public Square," and site of Kent County's first courthouse from 1838 to 1844, the park was given its current name in 1872, around the time that the wooden bandstand at its center was built. The park's benches and graveled walks make it a popular spot for a stroll, a rest, or just a breath of fresh air at the edge of downtown.

50

An ornate fountain went up in place of the old bandstand in 1890. This eventually was itself replaced in 1926 by a reflecting pool and memorial pylons commemorating the city's World War I armed services dead. The pylons were incorporated into the World War II and Korean War monument dedicated in 1957, at the time the square was renamed Veterans' Memorial Park. Additional markers on either side of the monument now also list names from the Vietnam War. Today surrounded by downtown, the park is still a pleasant green oasis at the city's heart.

51

Proceeding east on Fulton, we glance southward down Jefferson Avenue, a distinguished residential street. Harvey P. Yale, an early settler and onetime postmaster, lived on the southwest corner from 1854 until last year, but his original house burned down in 1868 and was replaced by this one. Down on the left side of the street, prominent lawyer and former state senator Lyman D. Norris lives in that first house with the bay window. Thomas Peck, one of the drugstore-owning Peck brothers, is his neighbor on the south. Hidden by trees are the riverstone Noyes Avery house and huge David Clay mansion on the Washington Street corner.

51

Commercial development has wiped out most traces of Jefferson's residential past. Only the former Norris and Peck houses still exist, occupied by offices and apartments and overshadowed by the Half Century, an apartment house built in 1905. The single-story Willard Building, with its peacock decorations, has stood on the Yale home corner since 1930. That four-story office building down on the Weston Street corner was opened in 1929 by the Litwin Tire Company as the biggest service station in Michigan. Past the 1940-vintage Fanatorium bowling alley stands the Grand Rapids Public Museum. After occupying the old Clay mansion, later owned by Nelson Howlett, for thirty-five years, the museum erected its present building on the site in 1938.

52

Ahead of us lies Fulton Street hill, seen here from the head of Jefferson Avenue. The "hill district" is the most fashionable neighborhood in town. Two of the oldest houses around are the stone cottage, built by Truman Lyon, at right and Abraham Pike's Greek revival-style home whose pillars barely show just beyond it. Both residences date from about 1845, when only woods surrounded them on all sides, and the pioneer Lyon and Pike families still live in them today. The big house across the street is only five years old and already has its second owner, banker A. J. Bowne. It's a home in mourning this spring — the Bowne's only child, a ten-year-old daughter, died in April after a brief illness.

The Bowne home went through several more owners before being torn down and replaced in 1916 by the massive stone First Methodist Church. The Masonic Temple went up next door about the same period. But the Lyon house, hidden beyond the Douma art supply store, still stands, occupied by doctors' offices. The Pike house survives, too, home to Design Quest since 1981, after serving for almost sixty years as first the Grand Rapids Art Gallery and later the Grand Rapids Art Museum. Fulton was widened to four lanes in 1957, taking out the rows of beautiful trees which once lined the hillside.

52

53

Partway up Fulton Street hill we pass Lafayette and look south. The home at left was built in 1849 by pioneer jeweler Aaron Dikeman. His son, outgoing mayor Edmund B. Dikeman, still lives there. Besides his political interests and the family jewelry business, Ed is widely known as an owner of race horses. Another former mayor, Martin Sweet, lives in the 1860-vintage house at right. Nearly seventy now, he was the richest man in town for a long time. His wealth hasn't declined any, but the fortunes of a few other lumbermen and capitalists have eclipsed his own. Sweet's hobby is breeding cattle on his farm just north of the city limits.

53

Martin Sweet and Edmund Dikeman were both ruined in the great financial crash of 1893. Dikeman moved to Chicago to start over, but Sweet lived on in near poverty in his home until he died in 1905. The house later was used as a music school, and one of the students, Arnold Gingrich (best known as the founding editor of *Esquire* magazine), used it as the setting of his 1935 novel, *Cast Down the Laurel.* The Women's City Club has been quartered there since 1928. The Dikeman house, converted from a private home to commercial use in 1950, is currently occupied by the Metternich-Cole interior decorating firm. The other old homes on South Lafayette have been torn down or turned into apartments.

54

Near the crest of the hill, at the northeast corner of Prospect and Fulton, stands the residence of Harry Widdicomb, one of the brothers who founded the great Widdicomb Furniture Company. Two other brothers, William and John, live on the same block where Harry built this mansion in 1883. With its solid mahogany floors, elegant crystal chandeliers, and beautiful hand-carved woodwork, the home ranks among the showplaces of Grand Rapids.

54

Harry Widdicomb, another victim of the crash of '93, sold his house that year to lumberman Delos A. Blodgett. The Blodgett family continued to live there until 1928. Before being torn down in 1935, the house spent its last years as the Kleynenberg School of Music. The lot stood vacant until the American Box Board Company erected this handsome brick office building in 1956. In recent years, much of the block has become part of the Davenport College of Business campus, and the building now houses the college's Peter A. Cook Administration Center.

55

Across Fulton Street is the home of another furniture magnate, George W. Gay, president of the huge Berkey & Gay Company. Built in 1883, this lavish residence stands on a historic site. Louis Campau, the fur trader who founded Grand Rapids, lived here from 1838 to 1862, in the big house which still can be seen behind the Gay mansion, where it has been moved and converted into a stable. Campau's place was the very first house to be built on the hill, when this now-fashionable neighborhood was only scrub oak tree and brush. Only fifty years later, the Gays' son, William, is to be married next month to Miss Netta Cole in a quiet ceremony. A new house for them will be built next door to the east.

Though the landscape around it has changed, the old home's exterior looks almost the same. After George Gay died in 1899, son William and his wife occupied the family mansion for the rest of their lives. In the early 1900s, they platted Gay Avenue through their property. Netta Gay put up a plaque on the home's west side to commemorate the old Campau home after the ramshackle old place had been torn down. The garage which replaced it, and the mansion itself, were converted into apartments a few years after Mrs. Gay's death in 1941. They stand today as handsome monuments to the gracious past of the neighborhood now known as Heritage Hill.

56

We've arrived out at Reeds Lake, three miles east of Grand Rapids, for a look at the O-Wash-Ta-Nong Boat Club boathouse. Remember, we passed their downtown headquarters earlier. The club was founded in 1885, "for the purpose of promoting social intercourse and stimulating athletic sports among the young men of our city, and to establish a much needed breathing spot for the families of its members during the heated term," to quote from its by-laws. This clubhouse is equipped with "rowing and pleasure boats, bowling alleys, billiard and pool tables, ladies' dining room, etc." Members also can enjoy swimming, fishing, picnic parties — even music recitals.

Unfortunately, even with five hundred members, the club couldn't sustain its taste for luxury. In 1895, three years after the O-Wash-Ta-Nongs went bankrupt, the building reopened under a similar organization, the Lakeside Club. A bigger, more elegant clubhouse later was built on the same spot. But history repeated itself, and this club also ended in financial trouble. Its quarters were twice destroyed by fire, the last time in 1918. Still, the boating tradition survives today at the site, a public launching ramp. Beyond it stand the docks of the marina operated by John "Bub" Rose, whose family has operated a business on the site since June 1901. To view the scene from exactly the same spot as before, of course, we'd have to be fifty feet out on the water.

This is the view south from the O-Wash-Ta-Nong boathouse veranda. Reeds Lake is still surrounded by farms, as it has been since the Reed brothers built their cabins beside it in 1934, but in the past twenty years the lake's west end has become a resort for the people of Grand Rapids. Two rail lines connect with the city, and several small steamboats like the one nearby carry passengers on pleasure outings. At boat landings, like Miller's over there, you can rent a rowboat or canoe for twenty-five cents an hour. The street railway company is promoting its park here as family-oriented, but saloons and gambling houses still give the lake area a rough reputation.

57

East Grand Rapids incorporated as a village in 1891, closing down its places of ill repute and allowing Reeds Lake to become, in time, the nucleus of a genuine family community. Cityhood came in 1929, and today there's not a farm to be seen. Still, the streetcar company's Ramona Park was a popular attraction until 1954. Its namesake steamboat didn't end its excursions for another year or two, docking right here where the old landing stood. Now the docks and boat liveries are gone, replaced by a pleasant park named for John A. Collins (1882-1982), a longtime mayor of East Grand Rapids and prominent figure in Kent County government. Beyond lie the local yacht club, city offices, and East Middle School.

58

Back from our jaunt to Reeds Lake, we observe one of the latest innovations in Grand Rapids, the new cable car line running up Lyon Street hill. Regular service started just a short time ago, on April 18, 1888. This is the company's powerhouse near Innes' Grove, between Union and Grand, where steam machinery pulls a cable of imported hemp rope set in a slot between the tracks. Grips on the passenger cars clamp onto the cable, which pulls them along. The cars' warning system is a bell attached to the rear axle — at each turn of the wheel the clapper hits the bell, making a cheerful clanging noise. Soon, seven miles of cable roadway will extend to all sides of the city, supplemented by horsecar feeders on some routes.

Cable cars turned out to be only a passing fad in Grand Rapids. The company merged with other local horsecar lines in 1890 to form the Consolidated Street Railway, and within a few years all its routes were converted to run electric trolleys. After holding the old powerhouse property for years, the street railway finally sold it for residential lots. By the late 1920s, not a trace of the building remained. The house at center was for over a half century the home of Frank J. Adams, a Polish immigrant who ran a tailor shop nearby and is still remembered affectionately for his services to several generations of Heritage Hill families.

59

Following the cable tracks westward, we come to the Union Benevolent Association Home and Hospital at the southwest corner of Lyon and College. The UBA, as it's known, started as a women's charitable group over forty years ago, and has grown into this modern facility which combines a home for the elderly on the first floor and a fully equipped hospital on the second and third. Begun in 1884 and opened early in 1886, the white brick and stone building cost over $31,000. A training school for nurses was established in connection with the association in 1886, and will soon graduate its first class.

The UBA eventually discontinued its senior citizen home to concentrate on hospital needs, but even then the old building gradually became overcrowded and outdated. In 1916, millionaire John W. Blodgett donated to the organization a new facility out in East Grand Rapids, where it has thrived ever since. His gift formed the foundation that has grown into the present Blodgett Memorial Medical Center. The antiquated building at Lyon and College was torn down, and a new Fountain School, replacing an earlier one on the site of Central High, went up on the lot in 1917. In the seven decades since, thousands of hill neighborhood children have received the basis of their education within its red brick walls.

60

Further west on Lyon Street, we find at Ransom Avenue an example of how the Grand Rapids landscape has been altered since pioneer times. This part of the hill was once much steeper, and it took considerable grading and filling to bring it down to the more moderate slope of today. Testifying to the change is the limestone David Leavitt mansion, built in 1858 atop the bluff and now standing high upon its lot, shored up by a system of stone retaining walls. Local historian Franklin Everett once quipped, "It is an easy thing for Leavitt to get down from his house on a slippery winter morning, but hard for an asthmatic man to get up there." Still, it offers a fine view of downtown and the new City Hall tower.

60

The Leavitt house had deteriorated to a shell of its former self, standing empty and "haunted" before it finally was torn down in the summer of 1950. The lower tier of stone retaining wall stood in place for another twenty-five years, and the lot was used for parking, until Grand Rapids Junior College's Gerald R. Ford Fieldhouse was built. People who cross today on the pedestrian overpass linking the athletic building with the JC Student and Community Center haven't a clue that the spot where they are walking high in the air was once ground level.

61

The Central High School, serving all students in town who want a diploma, has stood since 1868 on Ransom just south of Lyon, where Grand Rapids' first stone schoolhouse was built in 1849. The class of '88 numbers forty-two graduates, spread among seven majors which all concentrate heavily on languages and classical studies. If we weren't here after hours, we could get the janitor to unlock the tower for us to enjoy the greatest view the city has to offer. But there's another site almost as good. We'll go next for a look across the valley from the bluff three blocks north of here.

61

After a new high school building went up beside it in 1892, the old structure was demoted to a grammar school. When Central High moved to its present site on Fountain Street in 1911, the 1868 building was torn down. Its successor served as a junior high and then, in 1924, became home to Grand Rapids Junior College. Now part of a campus covering several city blocks, today's JC Learning Center — the fourth educational building to stand on this spot — represents Grand Rapids' unchanging commitment to the future, as symbolized in the education of its young people.

62

Here's our final vista — the Grand River valley, seen from the backyard of Civil War General Ambrose Stevens' house, on the bluff north of Hastings Street. Below us lies a fifteen-acre area rebuilt after the great fire of 1873, which destroyed nearly a hundred buildings north of Bridge Street. Across the river, we see the spires of St. Mary's and Second Street Methodist churches, and the tower of Union High School, left of the dam where we once looked back at this spot. Perhaps, even though to a sharp eye the shadows indicate high noon, we should imagine a glorious sunset in the distant sky, marking the end of our day's journey through Grand Rapids, then and now.

The view still holds a charm that no picture can quite convey. U.S. 131 has changed the face of the west riverbank, but St. Mary's still shows clearly, as does the domed Basilica of St. Adalbert, at right. On this side of the river, many old houses were demolished for the North Division Avenue extension in 1932 along the base of the hill, and others for the Gerald R. Ford Freeway (I-196), completed in 1964. The Grand Rapids Press building nestles south of the expressway, and on its north side, factories now fill the land down to the river.

As we follow the concrete ribbon winding into the sunset, just think: Wouldn't it be fun to come back in another hundred years and see what's happened to this town? Grand Rapids, Michigan — an American city, holding much in common with any other. And yet, past or present, it's always a very special place.

The Grand Rapids Historical Commission

John H. Logie, chairman
Francisco Vega, vice chairman
Margaret Snow, secretary

Micki Benz   Albert Steil
Mary Edmond   Anthony Travis
Harold Dekker   James VanVulpen
Leo W. Graff, Jr.   Mary Alice Williams
June Horowitz   Ronald Yob

Jenny Siweck, student member

James VanVulpen has gained a reputation as one of the leading experts on the history of Grand Rapids and its surroundings. His articles on many facets of the area's past have appeared in *Wonderland,* the *Grand River Valley Review* and *West Michigan Magazine.* In addition to his award-winning book, *A Faith Journey,* he has collaborated with Gordon Olson on *Peninsular Club: 1881-1981,* and with Reinder VanTil on *A Century of Caring.* He also provided much of the research for Gerald Elliott's *Grand Rapids: Renaissance on the Grand.* VanVulpen's writings have captured the color, humor, pathos, scandal, and inspiration of one Midwestern city's progress, making old times come alive for the modern reader.

Formerly a staff member of the local history department at the Grand Rapids Public Library, he became a free-lance consulting historian in 1980. His many projects since then have ranged from the research and writing of histories for notable buildings, businesses, and other institutions to assisting in the formation of the city's archives to his recent identification of thousands of historic photographs in the Public Museum's collection.

During his years as an officer and trustee of the Grand Rapids Historical Society, he edited the society's monthly paper, the *Grand River Times,* and has been associate editor of its magazine, the *Grand River Valley Review,* since 1983.

Rex D. Larsen has been a photojournalist for the *Grand Rapids Press* since 1977. He is widely known locally and throughout the state for his extraordinary newspaper photography and for his versatile photo reportage.

During his eleven years at the paper, Larsen, 32, has won numerous state and national awards for his work. In 1985, he was named by the Michigan Press Photographers Association as runner-up for the Michigan Photographer of the Year award. His many and diverse assignments have included photographing Pope John Paul II and Muhammed Ali and covering the Boston Marathon and the New York City fashion scene.

Self-taught as a photographer, Larsen studied arts and media at Grand Valley State University.

Primarily a photographer of people, Larsen, as he worked on *Grand Rapids Then and Now,* found a different kind of challenge in documenting the evolution of Grand Rapids and its urban structures.

"The changes in the buildings, in the landscape, spoke to me about the people who built a growing city. It told me about the character of the changing community."